Davis, Gibbs

Wackiest White House Pets

Pets

DATE DUE

WACKIEST

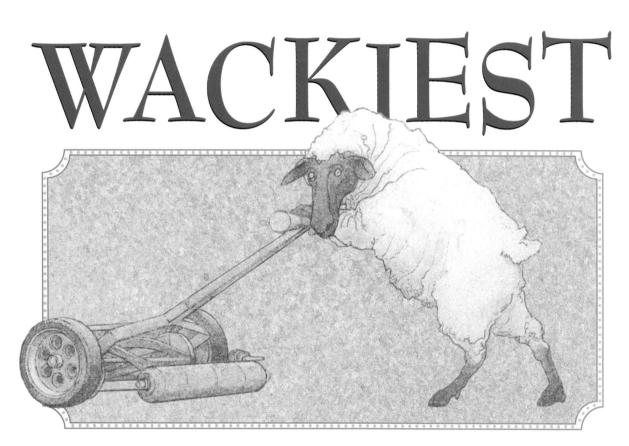

WHITE HOUSE PETS

WACKIEST
WHITE HOUSE PETS

BY GIBBS DAVIS

ILLUSTRATED BY DAVID A. JOHNSON

SCHOLASTIC PRESS • NEW YORK

★ ★ ★

LIBRARY OF CONGRESS CATALOGING-IN-PUBLICATION DATA

Davis, Gibbs. Wacky White House pets / by Gibbs Davis; illustrated by David A. Johnson.—1st ed. p. cm.

Summary: Describes the various kinds of pets, including grizzly bears and alligators, kept at the White House by various presidents from George Washington to George W. Bush.

1. Presidents—United States—Pets—Anecdotes—Juvenile literature. 2. Presidents—United States—Biography—Anecdotes—Juvenile literature. [1. Presidents—Pets.] I. Johnson, David A. 1951– ill. II. Title.

E176.48 .D38 2004   636.088'7'09753—dc22   2003020480

ISBN 0-439-44373-3

10 9 8 7 6 5 4 3 2 1   04 05 06 07 08

Printed in Singapore   46 ◆ First edition, October 2004

Artwork rendered in watercolor and colored pencil on paper.

The text is set in Caslon 540. Book design by David Caplan

We gratefully extend our thanks to Rex Scouten, former curator of the White House and namesake of Ronald Reagan's King Charles spaniel, Rex, and to Diane Nesin for their meticulous fact-checking of the manuscript.

★ ★ ★

To Dianne Hess, Top Dog Editor
– G. D.

To Ann, Stan, Adam, and Andy
– D. A. J.

Welcome to the White House Menagerie

Throughout the centuries, around four hundred pets have lived in the White House. Some were ordinary. Some were not. You might wonder how all of these creatures found their way to 1600 Pennsylvania Avenue.

A few pets arrived with their presidents. A handful simply wandered onto the White House lawn. One even turned up in the mail! But the wildest, wackiest pets were often gifts from kings, queens, and foreign officials. When even the White House's 132 rooms couldn't contain a restless elephant or a high-jumping wallaby, they were donated to Washington's nearby zoo. But most pets remained to live with the president's family.

Years ago, presidential pets were also practical. The White House lawn was home to farm animals such as cows, horses, sheep, goats, and chickens. These hard-working pets gave milk, butter, and eggs, trimmed the grass, and provided transportation for the First Families.

Times change, but one thing remains the same: Like us, presidents and their families love their pets—no matter how wacky—because, after all, pets make a house a home.

Even though many wacky pets have passed through the White House gates, this book will introduce you to some favorites—my vote for the Wackiest White House Pets.

—G.D.

CLEANEST TEETH

George Washington was the first president of the new United States. He had to decide what the job of president would be. After the Revolutionary War, General Washington was so popular that some people wanted him to be king. Washington helped America grow from thirteen separate colonies into a free nation.

"The Father of His Country" needed to be as stubborn as a mule. So it's no surprise that he created a line of "supermules." (A mule is a cross between a jackass and a mare.) The king of Spain wanted to help the president, so he offered Washington two of his best jackasses.

★ ★ ★

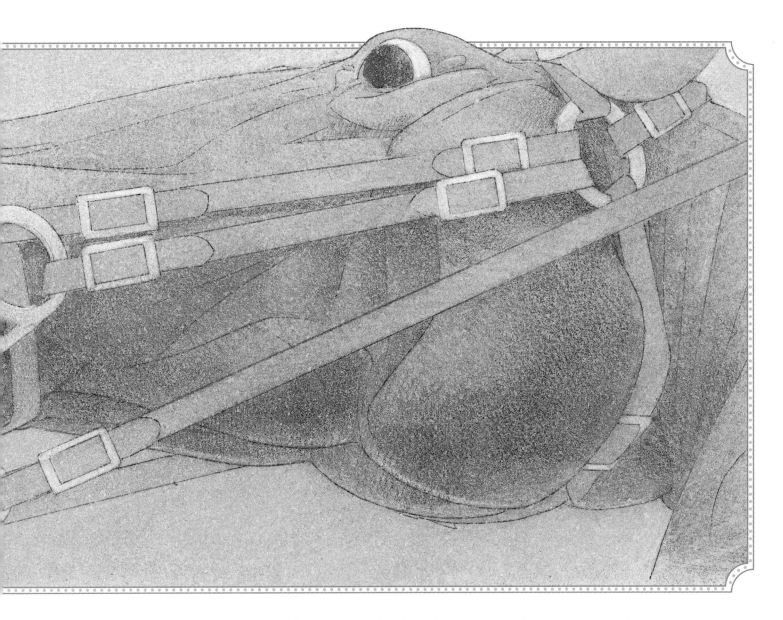

Of all our presidents, Washington was the best horseman. His horses were the most pampered pets in the country. Before riding, the president insisted the horses be polished from head to hoof. Even their teeth were brushed! He probably didn't want them to lose their teeth as he had: By age fifty-seven, he had only one tooth left and wore a set of false ones!

Washington had almost forty hounds. He treated them like members of the family. Each dog had a name to fit its personality, like Sweetlips, Tipler, or Madame Moose. A huge French hound named Vulcan had an appetite as big as he was.

One time Vulcan sniffed a freshly cooked ham on Martha Washington's dinner table. Opening his great jaws, Vulcan grabbed the ham and ran. Safe inside his kennel, the hungry hound gorged himself on the president's dinner.

The first First Pets never lived on the White House grounds—but they had a good reason: The White House hadn't been built yet! New York City was our nation's first capital (Philadelphia followed, then Washington, D.C., today's capital).

★ ★ ★

MOST GRIZZLY

President Thomas Jefferson had a brilliant, curious mind. Before he became president, he wrote the Declaration of Independence. As president, he doubled the size of America by buying the massive Louisiana Territory. In 1804, Jefferson sent the explorers Meriwether Lewis and William Clark on their long expedition to explore the wilds of the West.

One day, an especially large crate arrived at the White House. Growling and scratching sounds came from inside. The famous explorers had sent Jefferson two grizzly cubs!

The animal-loving president liked the young grizzlies so much, he decided to build them a cage on the South Lawn so they could be seen by the public. Jefferson often joined his growing cubs for walks around the garden. Jefferson's enemies made fun of his choice of pets. They called the White House grounds "the President's Bear Garden."

Jefferson was a true democrat. The author of the Declaration of Independence not only believed in equal rights for people, he believed in equal rights for animals, too. That included his feathered friends.

The president owned several mockingbirds. Dicky, his favorite, was allowed to fly free in the president's study. Jefferson and Dicky often performed duets. The president played the violin while Dicky whistled along. One of his many tricks was pecking bits of food from between Jefferson's lips. The amazing mockingbird could imitate almost any sound. He could even bark like a dog!

At bedtime, Jefferson's constant companion hopped up the White House stairs after him, one step at a time.

This pint-sized president didn't look much like a great leader. But you can't tell a president by his height. (At five feet four inches, James Madison was our shortest president.) Despite his protests, Madison is known as "the Father of the Constitution," the most influential thinker behind the government we still use today.

The short, white-haired president and his much younger, blooming wife made an odd-looking couple. But an even stranger-looking pair was First Lady Dolley Madison and her pet parrot.

Whoever said "birds of a feather flock together" must have had the president's colorful wife and her equally colorful green parrot in mind. A popular White House hostess, Dolley was called the "Queen of Washington City." She presided at the first Inaugural Ball, and her talking parrot was the star attraction at her many elegant parties. Wearing a tall, feathered turban, Dolley often entertained with her famous parrot perched on her shoulder. (In fact, Dolley was the White House hostess even before her husband became president. At a party during Jefferson's administration, Dolley introduced her guests to a new dessert—ice cream!)

During the War of 1812, the British invaded America. When British troops set fire to the White House, Dolley was forced to flee with just a handful of possessions. Fortunately, the First Lady was cool in a crisis. With just minutes to spare, Dolley decided what to take— the Declaration of Independence, a famous portrait of George Washington, and last but not least, her adored parrot!

Parrots live long lives, and Dolley's parrot was no exception. The celebrated parrot outlived both the president and the famous First Lady.

SNAPPIEST PET

President John Quincy Adams had lots of ideas about improving things like roads, canals, and schools. He had a hard time getting his improvements made, though. No one would say he had an easy time in the White House. Maybe that's why he was so understanding when an alligator came to visit.

In the summer of 1826, the alligator arrived with the president's good friend, the Marquis de Lafayette. The French war hero was the first celebrity to visit the White House. And the alligator was the first pet of its kind to ever slither across the White House steps. (Later on, President Herbert Hoover's son was given two alligators.)

For two months the green, scaly, sharp-toothed pet lived in the White House's giant East Room. Visitors who wandered in got a big surprise. They came running out with alligator jaws snapping at their heels!

Like his reptilian guest, Adams was a good swimmer. Early each morning the president went skinny-dipping in the Potomac River.

After a sad farewell ceremony, Lafayette and his alligator finally departed. The president and First Lady waved good-bye as they watched their visitor's green tail slide out of sight. See ya' later, alligator!

The Adams family also had the smallest pets in the White House. First Lady Louisa Adams raised silkworms and fed her tiny pets mulberry leaves. The silkworms thanked her by spinning the finest silk, which she wound herself. It was then sewn into luxurious gowns for the fashionable First Lady.

★ ★ ★

TINIEST DOG

Franklin Pierce didn't really want to be president. His friends nominated him. Tragedy followed him into the White House. Just before his inauguration, his third son died in a railroad accident.

It was a difficult time for our country, too. Everyone was arguing about slavery. Tensions between the North and the South were increasing. By the end of Pierce's term, the nation was hurtling toward the Civil War. Perhaps the president took some small comfort in his pocket-sized pet.

★ ★ ★

Two tiny "sleeve dogs" had sailed all the way from the Orient to America on Commodore Matthew Perry's flotilla. (The U. S. had just opened trade with Japan.) Perry had brought lots of other presents from Japan, but the president only had eyes for the diminutive dogs. It was easy to see why.

One of the dogs stayed on at the White House, but Pierce gave the other to Jefferson Davis. Davis would later become the president of the Confederacy. His new dog, named Bonin, was so tiny, he could sit on a saucer. With a head the size of a bird's, and large popped eyes, the bite-sized pup traveled in style through Washington's high society, tucked into Davis' pocket!

BIGGEST EARS

President James Buchanan was too old and cautious to make hard decisions. The nation was divided over slavery, and Buchanan refused to take sides. Seven Southern states ended up leaving the Union. They set up their own Confederate States of America.

Buchanan was the only president never to marry. His married friends were worried that the bachelor president might be lonely in the White House, so they were always sending him animals to keep him company.

The king of Siam presented Buchanan with a herd of elephants. They were the first White House pets to arrive with their own trunks! However, some animals were too big to live in the White House, so the president wisely decided to donate them to the local zoo. After all, elephants are the symbol for the Republican Party, and Buchanan was a Democrat!

One of the president's friends decided to send him a more patriotic pet—a pair of bald eagles. (This majestic bird is on the presidential seal.) However, they were sent to live at Wheatland, President Buchanan's Pennsylvania home. By day, the disappointed eagles walked the grounds. At night, they slept in twin cages on the back porch.

Buchanan owned one of the biggest dogs ever to live in the White House, a Newfoundland named Lara. At one hundred seventy pounds, the huge Newfie looked more like a bear than a dog. Lara became famous in Washington for her ability to lie still for hours, one eye open and one eye closed. The president and Lara must have made an interesting pair. Buchanan was nearsighted in one eye and farsighted in the other. He made up for it by always cocking his head to the left.

LUCKIEST PET

Few presidents achieved as much in their terms as Abraham Lincoln. He led the country during the bloody Civil War. He also issued the Emancipation Proclamation, which officially ended slavery in the rebel states. Times were hard for Lincoln during this difficult period in history. But he had a loving family, including two young sons, Tad and Willie. Along with their pets, these mischievous boys never failed to raise their father's spirits.

Honest Abe was the first president in office to wear a beard. However, he wasn't the only one in the White House with whiskers. Lincoln's youngest son, Tad, owned a pair of goats, Nanny and Nanko. Like Tad, the frisky goats were given full run of the White House. Tad liked to hitch the goats to chairs for racing carts. President Lincoln was amused by his son's pranks. But Mrs. Lincoln wasn't laughing. Tad liked to charge through his mother's formal parties.

One day Lincoln had an appointment in the city. He decided to take Tad and his goats along for the ride. Lincoln's assistant was shocked. He refused to sit next to the barnyard animals. (Guess who rode in the carriage and who stayed behind?)

Another time, Nanny was missing. Finally, Mary Ann Cuthbert, the chief housekeeper for the White House, found naughty Nanny. She was curled up in the middle of Tad's bed, chewing her cud.

In 1863, friends sent the Lincolns a live turkey for Thanksgiving dinner. Tad named him Jack, and he became a favorite pet. When Tad discovered Jack's fate, he burst into his father's office. Tad begged for Jack's life. President Lincoln listened carefully to his son. Then he wrote the lucky turkey a presidential pardon.

MOST SECRET PETS

Vice President Andrew Johnson never expected to become president. But when President Lincoln was assassinated, the vice president had no choice. Now that the Civil War was over, it was Johnson's job to restore the Union. He had a hard time. When Congress tried to impeach him, the president must have felt as if he didn't have a friend in the world—except for his secret pets.

One summer evening President Johnson let his favorite secretary, William Moore, in on a secret. He told him how he had discovered his new little pets. The night before, he had found some mice scurrying about, looking for food in his room. The president had left the little creatures a handful of flour.

"I am now filling the basket for them tonight," the president confided.

The next day the secretary asked President Johnson about his tiny friends.

"The little fellows gave me their confidence," the president said. "I gave them their basket and poured some water into a bowl on the hearth for them."

Andrew Johnson didn't like to see any creature go hungry. Perhaps he remembered from his childhood what it felt like to have an empty stomach. Johnson's parents were so poor, they couldn't afford to send him to school. Soon after the future president married his wife, Eliza, she taught him to read and write.

President Johnson liked to help the poor and the weak. It didn't matter if they were mice or men!

BIGGEST MENAGERIE

Theodore Roosevelt charged into the twentieth century. He was the first president to fly in an airplane, ride in a car, and submerge in a submarine. But this robust president never lost his love of nature. He saved millions of acres of wilderness. However, no place was more full of wildlife than the president's own house. Theodore Roosevelt had more than forty pets!

His teenage daughter, Alice, wanted an attention-getting pet. Her garter snake was named Emily Spinach because it was as green as spinach and as thin as Alice's Aunt Emily. Alice loved attending elegant parties with Emily Spinach. She would wait for a quiet moment, crack open her purse, and let Emily slither out. The president's daughter would

★ ★ ★

laugh as she watched the ladies race for the door, screaming.

Emily wasn't the only Roosevelt who liked snakes. Once, her brother Quentin barged into the Oval Office with a bag full of squirming snakes. When he dropped them onto a table to hug his father, chaos broke out. The five-foot king snake attacked the other snakes. The senators scrambled for safety as the reptiles did battle.

Nothing could separate the six Roosevelt children from their beloved pets. When Archie was sick in bed with the measles, his brothers knew how to cheer him up. They sneaked his calico pony, Algonquin, into the White House elevator and up to Archie's bedroom. There was just one problem: Algonquin was a vain little pony, and there was a mirror in the elevator. The pony fell in love with his own reflection, so the boys had a hard time pulling him out.

No pet was turned away from the Roosevelt zoo—including a one-legged rooster. Wilder pets such as a lion, a hyena, five bears, and a zebra were sent to live at their summer White House in Oyster Bay, Long Island!

★ ★ ★

At more than three hundred thirty pounds, William Taft was our largest president. Despite his size, Taft disappeared behind the larger-than-life figure of the previous president, Teddy Roosevelt. No matter how hard Taft tried, everyone liked Roosevelt better. At least President Taft could comfort himself with a glass of the fresh milk he loved.

Taft enjoyed fine food and fresh milk so much, he brought his own cow to the White House. Mooly Wooly was her name. (There were no dairy companies to deliver milk in those days. Cows were considered both practical and gentle pets.)

Poor Mooly Wooly's milk wasn't up to the president's standards. Mo-o-o-ove over, Mooly Wooly. A handsome Holstein named Pauline Wayne quickly replaced her. When Pauline wasn't being chased across the White House lawn by eleven-year-old Charlie Taft, she was busy producing milk for the president.

Taft hired a man just to look after Pauline. Every day he brought Pauline's milk to the White House kitchen. And every day the president gulped down glass after glass of her creamy fresh milk. In return, the prized cow got to sleep in the garage next to the president's elegant cars. (The horse stables had been converted to a garage.) Taft was the first president to buy automobiles for the White House.

Pauline wasn't the first cow to graze on the White House lawn. Sadly, she was the last. Unlike the cows, Taft's story had a happy ending. After he left office, he was appointed Chief Justice of the Supreme Court, his dream job, and lost ninety pounds.

BEST GARDENER

Aformer college professor, Woodrow Wilson was a man of ideas. He fought hard to
help the country win World War I. He fought just as hard to keep world peace
with his League of Nations. Though the League ultimately disbanded, Wilson's idea for a
world organization of nations does exist. It is called the United Nations.

During World War I, times were hard for Americans. All the young men were off fighting.
Who was going to mow the White House lawn? President Wilson had an idea. He would set an
example for government rationing. As part of the war effort, he brought in a flock of grass-eating
sheep. He also brought in a tobacco-chewing ram named Old Ike. (A ram is a male sheep.)

Old Ike and his patriotic sheep did their job. They grazed on the White House lawn until it was trim. There was just one problem: The hungry sheep ate the White House flowers, too!

Old Ike became a popular figure. He was rarely seen without a wad of tobacco between his teeth, juices running down his beard. But Ike was polite. He always cleaned up after himself. After he was finished chewing a wad, he swallowed it!

After the war ended, Old Ike left the White House lawn. But a bit of him returned: It was a blanket woven from the old ram's wool.

World War I was a time of plots and spies under every bed. So when the White House staff heard a loud tapping noise, they suspected spies at work. Could it be a secret code? When someone stepped out onto the roof to get some fresh air, they found their spy. A woodpecker was hammering away at the copper gutters!

★ ★ ★

MOST PAMPERED

Calvin Coolidge was president during the prosperous 1920s. It was called "the Roaring Twenties" because many Americans enjoyed a wild and extravagant lifestyle. Coolidge was not a man of his time. Nicknamed "Silent Cal," he had a quiet way of governing the country. However, he had no trouble communicating with animals.

One Thanksgiving the Coolidge family received a raccoon intended for their dinner table. President Coolidge took one look into her shiny brown eyes and named her Rebecca. Rebecca and the president became fast friends. He built her a special house outside the Oval Office. During the day she waddled up and down the White House halls. (She liked

★ ★ ★

to unscrew lightbulbs and unpot palms.) Most nights the president could be found walking his bushy-tailed pet on a leash.

When the White House was being repaired, the president's family had to move out. Poor Rebecca was left behind. The president worried about his people-loving pet and took action. He ordered the presidential limousine to pick up Rebecca and return her to the Coolidge family. After all, she was the First Raccoon!

Rebecca was not Coolidge's only wacky pet. There were also two white collies. Rob Roy was the president's dog. Mrs. Coolidge's favorite was Prudence Prim. The First Lady liked to sew matching floppy hats that she and her pooch would wear to White House garden parties.

Mrs. Coolidge hated to see any pet caged, including her flock of birds. Unfortunately, a big mynah bird's favorite perch was on top of the maid's head while she did her housework!

★ ★ ★

MOST SUSPICIOUS

John F. Kennedy was the youngest man ever elected president. The popular president and his stylish wife, Jackie, captivated the nation. During Kennedy's brief time in office he launched the space race. He also founded the Peace Corps to aid developing countries. Americans were fighting for their civil rights at home while the Cold War continued abroad.

During the Cold War, the Soviet Union and the United States didn't trust each other. The United States suspected everything that came from the Communist Soviet Union. Spies were everywhere. So when the president's daughter, Caroline, received a little dog from Soviet Premier Nikita Khrushchev, everyone was suspicious.

The little white dog was named Pushinka. (*Pushinka* means "fluffy" in Russian.) Pushinka was already a celebrity. Her mother, Strelka ("little arrow"), had been one of the first dogs sent into space. The Secret Service agents were suspicious of the fluffy little white dog. Was she a spy, too? The Russian dog didn't have fleas. But did she have other bugs? Pushinka was checked for secret microphones and spying devices. She passed the test with flying colors.

When Pushinka first saw the Kennedy's Welsh terrier, Charlie, it was puppy love. Soon, they had four pups. President Kennedy called them "pupniks."

The Kennedys received another unusual pet. This one was from a magician. It was a rabbit named Zsa Zsa. The talented bunny could play the first five bars of "The Star-Spangled Banner" on a toy golden trumpet!

BEST SWIMMER

Ronald Reagan was the oldest man ever elected president. He was also a former actor, appearing in over fifty films. Fearful of Communism, the president spent millions of dollars building up the military.

Everyone has a fish story. But only one president had a First Fish.

Reagan was recovering from an assassination attempt when he received something fishy in the mail. A ten-year-old boy had sent the president a goldfish in a plastic bag filled with water!

It didn't take long for the First Fish to get into the swim of things. The tiny White House resident was given a place of honor in a tank bearing the presidential seal.

Like the First Fish, the president was a powerful swimmer. As a young man, Reagan worked as a lifeguard during summer vacations on the Rock River in Illinois. He put a notch in a log every time he saved a person from drowning. In seven summers as a lifeguard, he made seventy-seven notches.

First Families often complain that living in the White House is a lot like living in a fishbowl. This is one fish who would know.

BEST-SELLING PET

George Herbert Walker Bush's inauguration in 1989 marked the two hundredth anniversary of the U.S. presidency. There had been many dramatic changes since our first president was in office. During Bush's term, Americans saw the collapse of Soviet Communism. The late twentieth century was also a glorious time for White House pets.

President Bush's springer spaniel, Millie, was voted "Ugliest Dog" in the Capital by *Washingtonian* magazine. Millie wasn't going to let sleeping dogs lie. She put paw to paper and set the story straight about her life in the White House.

Millie dictated 141 pages of her best-selling "dogobiography" to former First Lady Barbara Bush. In it, the famous First Dog recalls her heavy White House schedule. She also describes sitting in on morning briefings, chasing squirrels, and playing in the White House flower beds. Not one to let fame go to her head, she didn't neglect her duties as First Dog. She also mothered six puppies while in office.

The president was grateful to Millie. The published pooch had given practically all of her first year's royalties (almost $900,000) to the First Lady's favorite charity—the Barbara Bush Foundation for Family Literacy. Still, President Bush was a little jealous that the media hound got so much attention.

In *Millie's Book*, the spaniel writes, "'I overheard the Bushes talking the other night. Some discussion about me keeping a lower profile.'"

Every First Pet knows when to let the president be top dog.

MORE WACKY PET FACTS

The number one presidential pet has always been the dog. (George Washington had almost forty). Some First Dogs have been more popular than their presidents. President Harding was regarded as one of the worst presidents ever, but his upstanding Airedale terrier, Laddie Boy, became a national celebrity. (He even had his own special chair to sit in at cabinet meetings.) President Franklin Roosevelt's beloved little black Scottie, Fala, became an international celebrity, joining FDR at important world peace-making meetings. He traveled abroad more than any other White House pet. Both top dogs received thousands of gifts, letters, and invitations from their fans.

Who had the most pets? No contest here. Teddy Roosevelt and his six "bunnies" (his pet name for his children) turned the White House into a zoo. Calvin Coolidge ran a close second.

People say pet owners look like their pets. At over three hundred pounds, William Howard Taft was our largest president and he had pet cows. John Quincy Adams was one of our smallest presidents and his household had the tiniest presidential pets—silkworms. Many presidents share the same personality traits as their pets. Teddy Roosevelt was playful like his rowdy menagerie; Coolidge was stubborn, loyal, and quiet like his raccoon; Jefferson and his mockingbird were clever and shy; Franklin Delano Roosevelt and his dog Fala had star qualities; and like his fish, Reagan was an expert swimmer. There were only forty-three presidents and around four hundred presidential pets. The White House is truly an animal house. Pets rule!

On the following pages are more White House Pets and facts about their owners. This list does not represent every presidential pet. However, it is an accurate and comprehensive list compiled from available information. Cast your vote for your own personal favorite at: *www.scholastic.com*.

1. GEORGE WASHINGTON (1789-1797)
NICKNAME: Father of His Country

A Revolutionary War hero, Washington became the first president of the United States. He fought to free America from British rule.

Horses: Nelson and Blueskin (used during the American Revolution), Rozinante (granddaughter Nellie Custis's horse), Samson, Steady, Leonidas, Traveller, and Magnolia

Dogs: Mopsey, Taster, Cloe, Tipler, Forester, Captain, Lady, Rover, Sweetlips, Searcher, and Madame Moose (fox hounds), Vulcan (one of five French hound dogs given as gifts by the Marquis de Lafayette)

Jackass: Royal Gift (an Andalusian donkey from Charles III, the king of Spain)

Parrot (belonged to Martha Washington)

2. JOHN ADAMS (1797-1801)
NICKNAME: Duke of Braintree

Adams was V.P. when he was elected president, and was the first to reside in the White House. He saved America from war with France and established an official U.S. Navy.

Horses: Cleopatra (his favorite) and several others

3. THOMAS JEFFERSON (1801-1809)
NICKNAME: Red Fox

Author of the Declaration of Independence, Jefferson fought for religious freedom and doubled the size of the U.S. by buying the Louisiana Territory from France.

Birds: Dicky (his favorite among his several mockingbirds), peacock, pheasant

Bears: Two grizzlies (a gift from explorers Lewis and Clark)

4. JAMES MADISON (1809-1817)
NICKNAME: Father of the Constitution

Madison adopted the Bill of Rights. He also declared war on Great Britain. During this war, the War of 1812, the British set fire to the White House.

Green Parrot (belonged to First Lady Dolley Madison)

Sheep

5. JAMES MONROE (1817-1825)
NICKNAME: Last of the Cocked Hats

Monroe warned European countries not to interfere in the affairs of North and South America; this became known as the Monroe Doctrine.

Dogs: sheepdogs, black spaniel (belonged to Monroe's granddaughter Maria)

6. JOHN QUINCY ADAMS (1825-1829)
NICKNAME: Old Man Eloquent

The brilliant son of President John Adams accomplished little as president. People were not ready for his advanced ideas to improve the country.

Alligator (stayed for two months, along with his owner, Marquis de Lafayette)

Silkworms (raised by First Lady Louisa Adams)

7. ANDREW JACKSON (1829-1837)
NICKNAME: Old Hickory

Born in a log cabin, Jackson was the son of a poor farmer. The famous soldier was popular with the working class. He was responsible for the notorious Indian Removal Act of 1830 which eventually led to the Trail of Tears.

Horses: Truxton (champion race horse), Emily, Lady, Nashville, Bolivia (racing fillies), Sam Patches (favorite wartime mount)
Ponies
Birds: Poll (a parrot who screamed curse words at Jackson's funeral), gamecock

8. MARTIN VAN BUREN (1837-1841)
NICKNAME: Little Magician
Economic depression raged with this unpopular president. Under his administration, fifteen thousand Cherokee were forced from their homeland in a journey called the Trail of Tears.

Tigers: Two Cubs (a gift from the Sultan of Oman)

9. WILLIAM HENRY HARRISON (1841)
NICKNAME: Old Tippecanoe
Harrison was the first president to die in office. He also served the shortest term. One month after being elected, he died of pneumonia.

Durham cow: Suki
Billy goat

10. JOHN TYLER (1841-1845)
NICKNAME: His Accidency
Tyler was the first vice president to become president after the death of the elected president. He had fifteen children. A supporter of slavery, Tyler was an outcast from his own party, the Whigs. Texas joined the Union during his term.

Horse: The General
Dogs: Two Italian wolfhounds, one greyhound
Birds: Johnny Ty (one of his several canaries)

11. JAMES POLK (1845-1849)
NICKNAME: Young Hickory
After winning the Mexican War, the U.S. gained more land. Now the country reached from the Atlantic to the Pacific Ocean.

Pets: Unknown (No one knows for sure, but chances are he owned at least one horse. Growing up, Polk learned to ride as soon as he could walk.))

12. ZACHARY TAYLOR (1849-1850)
NICKNAME: Old Rough and Ready
A Mexican War hero, Taylor was a famous soldier. He did not want the new territories to become slave states, but he died too soon to act on his conviction.

Horse: Old Whitey (Taylor's wartime mount)

13. MILLARD FILLMORE (1850-1853)
NICKNAME: Last of the Whigs
Fillmore didn't work hard enough against slavery, so the North voted him out of office. He established shipping trade with Japan.

Pets: Unknown (However, he must have liked animals. Fillmore was a founding member and president of the Buffalo Chapter of the

American Society for the Prevention of Cruelty to Animals.)

14. FRANKLIN PIERCE (1853-1857)
NICKNAME: Handsome Frank
As people continued to argue over slavery, a bloody battle broke out in a conflict called "Bleeding Kansas." Pierce made many enemies.

Dog: Two sleeve dogs including Bonin (gifts from Commodore Matthew Perry)

15. JAMES BUCHANAN (1857-1861)
NICKNAME: Ten-Cent Jimmy
Seven southern states left the Union under Buchanan, the only bachelor president, and he did nothing to stop them.

Elephants (a gift from the king of Siam)
Bald eagles
Dog: Lara (Newfoundland)

16. ABRAHAM LINCOLN (1861-1865)
NICKNAME: Honest Abe
Lincoln led the North during the bloody Civil War. This legendary president restored the Union and ended slavery.

Goats: Nanny and Nanko (belonged to Tad)
Turkey: Jack (belonged to Tad)
White Rabbits
Ponies (belonged to Tad and Willie)
Cat (and a litter of kittens)
Dog: Jip (Lincoln's dog), Fido (yellow-brown mongrel, shared with another Springfield family); and other dogs

17. ANDREW JOHNSON (1865-1869)
NICKNAME: Tennessee Tailor
The first president to be impeached, Johnson was saved from being thrown out of office by one vote. He bought Alaska from Russia.

Mice
Jersey Cows

18. ULYSSES S. GRANT (1869-1877)
NICKNAME: Uncle Sam
A popular Northern general in the Civil War, Grant was not experienced in politics. His dishonest administration caused many scandals.

Horses: Including Jeff Davis (his wartime mount), Butcher Boy, Cincinnatus (a saddle horse), Julia (a racer), Egypt and St. Louis (carriage horses), and Jenny and Mary (Nellie Grant's mares)
Shetland ponies: Reb and Billy Button
Dogs: Including Faithful (Jesse's dog, a Newfoundland that was appointed White House steward)
Parrot (belonged to Jesse Grant)
Gamecocks (belonged to Jesse Grant)

19. RUTHERFORD B. HAYES (1877-1881)
NICKNAME: His Fraudulency
Hayes won the presidential election by one vote. Many people said it wasn't fair. He was the first president to use a telephone in the White House.

Goats (belonged to his grandson, Scott)
Dogs: Duke (English mastiff), Hector (Newfoundland), two shepherd dogs, Grim

(Scott's greyhound)
Birds: Canaries, mockingbird, pigeon
Cat: Siam (Siamese)
Jersey cows
Carriage horses

20. JAMES GARFIELD (1881)
NICKNAME: Preacher President
Garfield was the third Civil War general to become president. After four short months in office, he was shot. He died two months later.

Dog: Veto
Fish
Horse: Kit (Molly Garfield's mare)

21. CHESTER ALAN ARTHUR (1881-1885)
NICKNAME: Elegant Arthur
Nobody expected much from Arthur. However, he worked hard to make the government more honest and he reformed the civil service system.

Pets: Unknown

22. GROVER CLEVELAND (1885-1889)
NICKNAME: Uncle Jumbo
Honest, hardworking Cleveland was the only president to serve two terms—not in a row—and the first to be married in the White House.

Dog: One-and-one-half-pound gift from a Milwaukee man, probably either a Japanese poodle or a Pekingese from China.
Birds: Mockingbird, canaries

23. BENJAMIN HARRISON (1889-1893)
NICKNAME: Little Ben

Grandson of the ninth president, Harrison tried to help U.S. businesses. He was the first president to use electricity in the White House.

Goat: Old Whiskers
Opossums: Mr. Reciprocity and Mr. Protection
Dog: Dash
Horses: Abdullah, Lexington, Billy, and John
Bird

24. GROVER CLEVELAND (1893-1897)
(see president #22)

25. WILLIAM MCKINLEY (1897-1901)
NICKNAME: Wobbly Willie
After winning the Spanish-American War, the U.S. gained Hawaii. Now the nation was a global power.

Parrot: Washington Post (Mexican double yellow-headed parrot)
Cats: Mother and her four kittens, including Valeriano Weyler, named after the governor of Cuba, and Enrique DeLome, namesake of the Spanish Ambassador to the U.S. (Angoras)

26. THEODORE ROOSEVELT (1901-1909)
NICKNAME: TR
A "hands-on" president, TR established the U.S. as a world power while protecting workers at home. He inspired "the Teddy bear."

Bear: Jonathan Edwards (and four others)
Lion
Wildcat
Coyote

Zebra

Lizard: Bill

Piebald rat: Jonathon

Kangaroo rat

Badger: Josiah

Pig: Maude

Guinea pigs: Dewey Senior, Dewey Junior, Dr. Johnson, Bishop Doan, Fighting Bob Evans, and Father O'Grady

Icelandic pony: Algonquin (a calico pony belonging to Archie)

Snakes: Emily Spinach (green garter snake belonging to Alice), five-foot king snake, black snake, gold-banded snake, and common grass snake (belonging to Quentin)

Cats: Slippers (the six-toed cat) and Tom Quartz

Dogs: Sailor Boy (Chesapeake retriever), Jack (terrier belonging to Kermit), Pete (Bull Terrier), Manchu (black Pekingese belonging to Alice), Skip (mongrel)

Birds: Barong Spreckle (a hen), Eli Yale (a blue macaw), one-legged rooster, barn owl, chicken, parrots, canaries, and an eagle

Flying squirrel

Rabbit: Peter

Hyena

Horses: Bleistein (Roosevelt's favorite), General and Judge (carriage horses), Renown, Roswell, Rusty, Jocko, Root, Grey Dawn, Wyoming, Yagenka

27. WILLIAM HOWARD TAFT (1909-1913)
NICKNAME: Big Bill
Taft worked hard to preserve federal law and to break up powerful trusts. He began the presidential tradition of throwing out the first ball of the baseball season.

Cows: Mooly Wooly, Pauline Wayne (last cow on the White House lawn)

28. WOODROW WILSON (1913-1921)
NICKNAME: Professor
After winning World War I, this idealistic president tried to convince the U.S. to join a world family called the League of Nations. In 1920, the Nineteenth Amendment to the Constitution gave all female U.S. citizens the right to vote.

Sheep

Ram: Old Ike (tobacco-chewing ram)

Cat: Puffins

Birds: Chicken, songbirds

29. WARREN HARDING (1921-1923)
NICKNAME: Wobbly Warren
Harding was the first president to speak on the radio. His administration was filled with dishonest men. He died suddenly before a big scandal broke. Some think he was murdered.

Dogs: Laddie Boy (an Airedale that sat in his own chair at cabinet meetings and had his own valet.), Oh Boy (bulldog)

Birds: Turkeys, Bob and other canaries (belonging to Mrs. Harding)

30. CALVIN COOLIDGE (1923-1929)
NICKNAME: Silent Cal
Coolidge's old-fashioned, honest values restored people's faith in the government. Businesses prospered, and the country got richer.

Raccoons: Rebecca and Horace

Antelope

Bear

Birds: Nip and Tuck (Hartz Mountain olive-green canaries), Snowflake (white canary), Enoch (goose), Old Bill (thrush), Goldy (unknown yellow bird), mockingbird, mynah bird, parrot, Do-Funny (trained tropical), flock of chickens (They stayed in the president's bathtub because there was nowhere else to put them.)

Bobcat: Smokey

Cats: Bounder, Blackie, and Tiger

Cow

Dogs: Palo Alto (bird dog), Boston Beans (bulldog), Blackberry and Tiny Tim (chows), Prudence Prim and Rob Roy (white collies), Ruby Rough (brown collie), Bessie (yellow collie), Calamity Jane (Shetland sheepdog), Peter Pan (terrier), Paul Pry (Airedale), King Kole (black Belgian police dog)

Donkey: Ebenezer

Pygmy hippos (mother and baby)

Lions: two cubs (gifts from the mayor of Johannesburg, South Africa)

Wallaby

31. HERBERT HOOVER (1929-1933)

NICKNAME: Chief

In 1929, the stock market collapsed, causing the Great Depression. Millions of homeless and unemployed Americans blamed Hoover. His efforts to aid the country came too little too late.

Opossum: Billy

Dogs: Big Ben and Sonnie (fox terriers), Glen (Scotch collie), Yukon (Eskimo dog), Patrick (Irish wolfhound), Eaglehurst Gillette (Irish setter), King Tut and Pat (police dogs), Weeje (elkhound)

32. FRANKLIN DELANO ROOSEVELT (1933-1945)

NICKNAME: FDR

FDR helped people without jobs during the Great Depression and led the U.S. during most of World War II. A victim of polio, he used a wheelchair and braces after age thirty-nine.

Dogs: Fala (a black Scottie and the most famous of all White House pets), Major (German shepherd), Meggie (Scotch terrier), Winks (Llewellyn setter), Blaze (mastiff belonging to Elliot Roosevelt), President (Great Dane), Tiny (English sheepdog), Pal and Dutchess (unknown breed)

33. HARRY TRUMAN (1945-1953)

NICKNAME: Man from Independence

Truman had atomic bombs dropped on Japan, quickly ending World War II. Fearful of the spread of Communism, he declared war on Korea.

Dogs: Mike (Irish setter belonging to daughter, Margaret), Feller (cocker spaniel)

Cat: Mike the Magicat

Goat: Dewey's Goat (named after Truman's presidential opponent, Thomas E. Dewey)

34. DWIGHT DAVID EISENHOWER (1953-1961)

Nickname: Ike

The popular World War II general ended the

Korean War. During the 1950s the U.S. was afraid of Communism. The space race began.

Dogs: Heidi (Weimaraner), Spunky (black Scottie)
Squirrels

35. JOHN FITZGERALD KENNEDY
   (1961-1963)
NICKNAME: JFK
The handsome young JFK was, at forty-three, the youngest man ever elected president. He started the Peace Corps and worked for equal rights. He raced with the Soviet Union to put a man on the moon.

Irish deer
Ponies: Macaroni (belonging to daughter Caroline), Leprechaun (belonging to son John, Jr.), and Tex
Horse: Sardar (belonging to Mrs. Kennedy, a gift from the president of Pakistan)
Hamsters: Billie and Debbie
Guinea pig
Cat: Tom Kitten (later renamed Tom Terrific)
Dogs: Charlie (Welsh terrier belonging to Caroline Kennedy), Clipper (German shepherd), Shannon (Irish spaniel, a gift from Ireland's prime minister), Wolf (Irish wolfhound), Pushinka (unknown species, a gift to Caroline from the Soviet premier along with her and Charlie's four pups: Butterfly, White Tips, Blackie, and Streaker)
Birds: Robin (canary), Bluebelle and Maybelle (parakeets)
Lamb
Rabbit: Zsa Zsa (the trumpet player)

36. LYNDON BAINES JOHNSON
   (1963-1969)
NICKNAME: LBJ
After Kennedy's sudden death, LBJ took office. Criticized for escalating the Vietnam War, he was a champion for equal rights and the poor.

Dogs: Yuki (mongrel), Old Beagle and pups Kim, Freckles, Dumpling, Little Chap, Him, and Her (beagles), Blanco (white collie), Edgar (unknown species, a gift from J. Edgar Hoover)
Hamsters
Lovebirds

37. RICHARD NIXON (1969-1974)
NICKNAME: Tricky Dick
The Vietnam War ended, three American astronauts landed on the moon, and Nixon opened friendly talks with China and the Soviet Union. Directly linked to the break-in of a Democratic party office in the Watergate Hotel, he was faced with impeachment and became the first U.S. president to resign from office.

Dogs: Checkers (cocker spaniel), Vicky (French poodle belonging to daughter Julie), Pasha (Yorkshire terrier belonging to daughter Tricia), King Timahoe (Irish setter)
Fish

38. GERALD FORD (1974-1977)
NICKNAME: Mr. Nice Guy
After pardoning Nixon for his part in the Watergate scandal, Ford became the first un-elected U.S. president.

Dog: Liberty and her eight pups including Jerry who went on to become a guide dog for the blind (golden retrievers)
Cat: Chan (Siamese)
Deer: Flag

39. JIMMY CARTER (1977-1981)

NICKNAME: Hot

New to politics, Carter had an informal public image. He preferred Jimmy to his given name, James Earl Carter, Jr. He led important peace talks between Israel and Egypt.

Cat: Misty Milarky Ying Yang (Siamese)
Dog: Grits

40. RONALD REAGAN (1981-1989)

NICKNAME: Dutch

The oldest elected president and a former actor, Reagan was known as "the Great Communicator." Fearful of the Soviets, he spent millions on military buildup. Though popular, he doubled the national debt.

Dogs: Rex (King Charles spaniel), Lucky (sheepdog), Scotch and Soda (black Scottish terriers), Victory (golden retriever)
Horse
Fish

41. GEORGE H. W. BUSH (1989-1993)

NICKNAME: Poppy

The Cold War ended, the Berlin Wall came down, and the Soviet Union and the U.S. were no longer enemies. The U.S. fought the Persian Gulf War.

Dogs: Millie, Fred, and their six puppies, including Ranger (springer spaniels)

42. WILLIAM JEFFERSON CLINTON (1993-2001)

NICKNAME: Bubba

During a time of peace and prosperity, Clinton focused on social reforms. He was impeached, but later acquitted by the Senate.

Cat: Socks (first White House pet with website)
Dog: Buddy (chocolate Labrador)

43. GEORGE W. BUSH (2001-)

NICKNAME: Dubya

A war against terrorism was declared after the worst foreign attack on U.S. soil.

Cats: Ernie and India
Dogs: Spot Fetcher Bush (Millie's puppy, an English springer spaniel), Barney (black Scottish terrier, whose two videos can be seen on the White House website)
Cow: Ofelia (a longhorn that lives at his ranch)

BIBLIOGRAPHY

Aikman, Lonnelle. *The Living White House*. Washington, D.C.: White House Historical Association with the National Geographic Society, 1991.

Barber, James. *Presidents*. New York: Dorling Kindersley, 2000.

Bush, Barbara. *Millie's Book: As Dictated to Barbara Bush*. New York: William Morrow, 1990.

Clinton, Hillary Rodham. *Dear Socks, Dear Buddy: Kids' Letters to the First Pets*. New York: Simon & Schuster, 1998.

Coulter, Laurie. *When John and Caroline Lived in the White House*. New York: Hyperion/Madison Press, 2000.

Davis, Kenneth C. *Don't Know Much About the Presidents*. New York: HarperCollins Publishers, 2002.

Greene, Carol. *Presidents*. Chicago: Children's Press, 1984.

Karr, Kathleen. *It Happened in the White House: Extraordinary Tales from America's Most Famous Home*. New York: Hyperion, 2000.

Kay, Helen. *The First Teddy Bear*. Owings Mills, MD: Stemmer House Publishers, 1985.

Kelly, Niall. *Presidential Pets*. New York: Abbeville Press Publishers, 1992.

Krull, Kathleen. *Lives of the Presidents: Fame, Shame (and What the Neighbors Thought)*. San Diego: Harcourt Brace & Company, 1998.

Rowan, Roy, and Brooke Janis. *First Dogs: American Presidents and Their Best Friends*. Chapel Hill, NC: Algonquin Books of Chapel Hill, 1997.

Rubel, David. *Scholastic Encyclopedia of the Presidents and Their Times*. New York: Scholastic Reference, 1994.

Seale, William. *The President's House*. 2 vols. Washington, D.C.: White House Historical Association with the National Geographic Society, 1986.

St. George, Judith. *So You Want to Be President?* (Illustrated by David Small). New York: Penguin Putnam Books, 2000.

Sullivan, George. *Facts and Fun About the Presidents*. New York: Scholastic Inc., 1987.

Truman, Margaret. *White House Pets*. New York: David McKay Company, Inc., 1969.

"If you want a friend in Washington, get a dog."
— *President Harry Truman*